Writing Great Characters in the First Ten Pages

SAN DIEGO STATE UNIVERSITY
25th Annual Writers Conference

WORKSHOP TRANSCRIPT
HOW TO ADAPT YOUR NOVEL INTO A SCREEN PLAY

BOOK 1

FRANK CATALANO

BOOKS BY FRANK CATALANO

Art of the Monologue
Monologues they haven't heard yet

The Creative Audience
The collaborative role of the audience in the creation of the visual and performing arts

White Knight Black Night
Short monologues for auditions

The Resting Place
a play

Autumn Sweet
a play

Rand Unwrapped
Confessions of a Robotech Warrior

Che Che
a screenplay

Short Monologues for Auditions

WRITING GREAT CHARACTERS IN THE FIRST TEN PAGES was first presented as part of the 25th Annual Writer's Conference sponsored by San Diego State University on February 6 through the 8th, 2009 at the Double Tree Hilton Hotel in Mission Hills, California. The following transcript was presented and recorded by Frank Catalano as part of the programs offered at the conference.

Writers of fiction and non-fiction and industry professionals from the publishing business primarily attended the 25th Annual Writer's Conference. Mr. Catalano's seminars focused upon those writers seeking to adapt their novels into screenplays. The complete list of seminar presentations by Frank Catalano for this conference is:

BOOK 1: WRITE GREAT CHARACTACTERS IN THE FIRST TEN PAGES

BOOK 2: WRITING ON YOUR FEET - IMPROVISATIONAL TECHNIQUES FOR WRITERS

BOOK 3: START YOUR STORY AT THE END

BOOK 4: THE FIRST TEN PAGES

BOOK 5: BOOK TO SCREEN

BOOK 6: ACTING IT OUT – IMPROVISATIONAL TECHNIQUES FOR WRITERS II

BOOK 7: WRITE GREAT DIALOGUE

CONTENTS

Writing Great Characters in the First Ten Pages

WORKSHOP INTRODUCTION

Good afternoon, my name is Frank Catalano and this is **WRITING GREAT CHARACTERS IN THE FIRST TEN PAGES**.

I hope you are all having a great time today at the 25th Annual Writer's Conference and what we are going to be working on today. What I'd like to do first is introduce myself and say a few words about who I am and then I want to see where you guys are with your individual projects. The trend has been mostly fiction writers but there might be a couple of screenwriters as well. In this seminar we are going to explore the process of presentation. You know, I just want to say this when you are working on the presentation of material; you always have to come up with kind of a nifty title. And so I want to look at this idea of *writing great characters in ten pages* and what that title means. What it really means as opposed to beyond what a title is. Okay, we will try to look today and try and give you kind of a working understanding of how to transition your novel into a successful screenplay - writing actively and how to get better at it. If you are a novelist, how can you transition what you have written within in a literary form into writing for the screen?

Now before I begin, I'm going to pass this around and it is not obligatory – you don't have to do it. But, if you want to provide your email, I will have an email version of what we will talk about today – some notes. I can send that to you and when I do send it to you, you will have my email address. So you can email me back if you have any questions. We will start it here and end it there. Put your first and last name on it as well. This way I will have it. Yes?

Audience member: "Are you a writing teacher?"

"Yes"

(Audience laughter)

Well actually, I park the cars over here.

(Audience laughter)

You know I was at Warner Brothers for many years and I will tell you what I did there in a minute. And when I said I worked at Warner Brothers, people would always ask: "What do you do there?" And, I would tell them… and I got really elaborate that I parked the cars and washed the cars. But none of that is true. Anyway, let me tell you what I do. I am a college professor. I've been at University of Southern California for thirty-four years…

(Audience laughter)

teaching at the School of Theatre (now School of Dramatic Arts as of 2012). I teach acting, writing and theatre and all different kinds of elements of presentational performance. I also teach Humanities courses that include visual and performing arts: painting, sculpture, film, television and audience studies. I do all of that. My acting classes are both on camera and stage. As a theatre producer/playwright I have had productions at the Beverly Hills Playhouse in Los Angeles and have had shows in New York and other places.

I've been at Warner Brothers (I've said that) and worked at quite a few other studios. Warner Brothers and Lorimar Productions probably the longest. I did various jobs including consultancies, packaging, marketing and writing. I had what is called a *first look writing agreement* at Warner Brothers for the development of motion pictures and television productions. Working at a movie studio is can be a great experience both good and bad. The good is the studio provides a framework to develop everything you write although they are not obligated to produce it. So you set up shop there, you write, you work with other writers sometimes. But, the hard part of that process is that not very much gets actually made. In a large studio universe, producing was something totally different than writing. I just primarily focused on the writing.

I am also an author. *I have two books out: ART OF THE MONOLOGUE (2007). It's a theatre book for actors with original monologues and a large section on monologue performance theory. I've also had plays produced and published. I have a new play being published right now and I have a brand new book coming out this month called THE CREATIVE AUDIENCE – THE COLLABORATIVE ROLE OF THE AUDIENC IN THE CREATION OF THE VISUAL AND PERFORMING ARTS (2009) and so it is not being sold in the lobby.

*Since this 2009 presentation, Frank Catalano has published the following books:

ART OF THE MONOLOGUE (2007)
THE CREATIVE AUDIENCE (2009)
WHITE KNIGHT BLACK NIGHT – SHORT
   MONOLOGUES FOR AUDITIONS (2010)
AUTUMN SWEET – A PLAY (2011)
THE RESTING PLACE – A PLAY (2011)
RAND UNWRAPPED – CONFESSIONS OF A
   ROBOTECH WARRIOR (2012)
CHE CHE – A SCREENPLAY (2013)
SHORT MONOLOGUES FOR AUDITIONS (2013)
MYTHS AND TANGOS (2014)

My new book (The Creative Audience) deals a subject I have really been thinking about and actually we are going to talk about it today. That is the creative role of the audience in the making of visual and performing arts. It takes into consideration the both the visual and performing arts including painting and advertising. But it also covers film, television and the Internet. How things are created today on the macro level almost in reverse. When someone comes up with a creative idea, it's really kind of tested first to see if the audience will respond positively to it. They do the same through polling in politics. Former president Bill Clinton's administration was very adept at formulating policies around the acceptance or rejection of public opinion. Many times his administration would poll certain policy ideas to see how the public would react to them. This is common practice today. Former president President Bush's administration, had a slightly different approach to policy, he had several core beliefs that he wanted to see formulated and he did what he felt he had to do despite public opinion. Today, leaders determine policy often by polling. They develop policy and then frame it in a certain way for public consumption to obtain the result they want to get. It doesn't mean they lie. It just means that information is just packaged a certain way. And it's going on right now, when we watch the news. Depending on "how" the information is presented determines how we react to it in the end. It also can be considered in writing – especially in what you guys are doing.

PAGE TO SCREEN

The presentation of your work to others is almost as important as the idea (the work) itself. That's what I was thinking of before I came here today to meet all of your. What would be the best "frame" to put this seminar in? WRITING GREAT CHARACTERS IN THE FIRST TEN PAGES? What does this title actually mean? Let's think of it this way. We have all probably been to McDonalds or Burger King?

(Audience laughter)

I know you have. You probably won't admit it.

(Audience laughter)

And what are you getting? We "hope" that it's a beef patty. Right? And why did we go there? Because eating fast good is a fast and inexpensive way to eat. We didn't go there for the atmosphere. Now let's take that same beef patty and place it in a really fancy restaurant. In Los Angles, we have Wolfgang Puck's Grill in Beverly Hills. Now let's take that same hamburger patty and maybe change the shape of it a little so it doesn't look like a patty. We add carrots, potatoes, garnish sauce and other things around it. Present it in soft amber lighting, candles, and violin music playing… and now that hamburger patty that was under a dollar costs thirty dollars.

(Audience laughter)

But what has changed? Nothing. The only thing that's changed is the frame that the "patty" has been placed within. And this is important to stress. It is not a lie in the sense that I'm not taking out the patty and putting it in my pocket and replacing it with a filet mignon steak. No, it's the same patty. What *has* changed is the point of view and the framework of the presentation. That is the most important thing. The idea remains the same. By extension, the process for writing characters or converting characters from a novel is quite the same thing. It's all how you frame them at the start of your story.

I want to explore the differences between the two mediums. So with that in mind, how many of you are active screenwriters?

(Audience member raising hand)

I've got one… I've got two. And you?

(Audience member: "Off and on…")

But you have written screenplays. Have any of your screenplays been put into production?

(Audience member: "No, but it's been work shopped.")

Okay. How about you?

(Audience member: "I'm going to make my own film.")

Great! Wonderful. And you know what? That's the future. When you go to Warner Brothers and other majors and they might tell you, "Well, we just don't know what to do with your project… it doesn't fit in… it just won't work for us."

Then there people, right out of film school, that don't know the rules (that's a good thing). They aren't aware of what they are supposed to do or not do because the schools they attend never prepare them that way.

(Audience laughter)

They go out and they create a short film, a trailer or series of webisodes on YouTube and now they have something tangible to show the world. The discussion can be quite different then. "I have four films up on YouTube or Vimeo and have 50,000 or 100,000 hits. Would you like to view it?" What are they actually looking at? Yes, a sample of the writer's work. But they are looking at much more. The work they view is a movie or series that would probably have never been made. So this is a very good way to go if you are developing your novel into a screenplay. You can do the same thing. You can put up portions of your work (trailers). When I say post, I mean shoot scenes or readings and put them up.

So, what do I want to say about writing great characters in the first ten pages? It's a catchy title. I'm going to be straight with you.

(Audience laughter)

It really should be WRITNG GREAT CHARACTERS FOR THE MEDIUM or WRITING GREAT CHARACTERS FOR A PRESENTATION. But then, you wouldn't come. But you are saying "What about the first ten pages?" Let's talk about that. Writing great characters, we all want to do that. That's a given... and we are primarily fiction writers (novels) and you have your characters set up in your books and within that medium, you have a certain methodology of development and narrative. You have the ability to to stop in the middle of a story and go into the childhood or a past event, which tells the reader something significant about your character. However, in film (and I will break down film into television and film) you don't have that luxury. There is a general framework in feature film writing of approximately how long the screenplay should be and then on the production side how long the final film should be in relationship to the audience expectation. How long is an audience willing to sit in a darkened theatre watching a particular film? Probably, two hours for a normal showing of a story and maybe longer say three hours for a larger subject like Gandhi (1982), Dances with Wolves (1990) or Titanic (1997). There is an expectation of run time here. In film, you can't meander off the main narrative for very long or risk losing your script reader or audience.

WHAT AN AUDIENCE
EXPECTS OF YOU

We're all an audience at some time or another. When you go to the movies and we all go, what would you think if I were to say to you – ask you – what is the appropriate run time for a motion picture? In other words, if you get all dressed up, walk out the door and you buy your ticket for an 8:00 PM showing and you attend the whole showing, when do you expect to return home? Assuming you don't stop somewhere after the movie.

(Audience response – two hours… about ten o'clock.)

Yes, ten o'clock. And what if you're going to the opera?

(Audience laughter)

Nobody here goes to the opera? Are you with me on that one?

(Audience laughter)

I went to the opera CARMEN at the Dorothy Chandler Pavilion (home of the Los Angeles Opera) with Placido Domingo conducting and I sat there with my daughter. After Act 1, Act 2, there was a short intermission and I said to her, "Honey that was great!" I thought it was over because two and half hours had passed. She smiled at me and said; "Dad, it's just the intermission."

(Audience laughter)

"There are another three acts." Three acts? So, I went straight to the bar.

(Audience laughter)

Okay, anyway… so there is a certain audience expectation, which is somehow attached to the medium in which a work of art (film, television show, novel) is presented. No one wrote this down. There are no traffic cops there if it is not followed. But there is an unstated expectation. Certain media or mediums evoke a specific audience expectation. There is some evidence typically in motion pictures that this is the case.

If we were to go back in time to let's say 1939 when 90 million people went to the movies every week. When you attended a movie in 1939, you looked up at the theatre marquee and it might have had a particular actor's name above the title. Something like "Judy Garland and Mickey Rooney in the MGM Sensation – THE WIZARD OF OZ." But above it all would be the name of the studio that owned the theatre – Paramount, Warner's, MGM/Lowe's, Fox or Universal. These were the five major studios at the time. My point is the production entity which might have been Paramount or Warners – any one of the big five owned the production of that film, hired (as contract employees) all the above the live (as non contract employees) and below the line creative people. They also owned one hundred percent of the distribution and owned the physical theatre – the brick and mortar building where the film was exhibited.

(New female audience member enters the room – but there are no seats. Catalano, provides his own.)

Here take mine. Chivalry is not dead.

(Audience laughter)

Why don't you sit right over here?

And they owned the physical theatres (brick and mortar), which meant... if the movie (run time) ran long, they didn't care. If the movie was bad, they didn't care.

(Audience laughter)

...of course they want the films to be good. But really, it didn't matter because they knew they had 90 million plus people a week going to the movies. No matter what.

(Audience laughter)

No, seriously... and it was given. They could put a chicken chasing a worm up on the screen and they knew they were going to make their numbers. Why? They owned the very seats the audience sat on. They owned the candy, the popcorn. They owned everything and were able to keep all of the money they made after costs. What about today?

Today, let's use the same example. Paramount is part of a larger corporation – Viacom that owns the studio, may own the distribution of a particular film. However, they no longer own the physical movie theatres. Studios had to give up ownership of exhibition (movie theatres) in 1948 by order of the Supreme Court (Paramount Decree). Movie theatres today are owned by exhibition entities independent of the producing company of a particular film. What this means is that all those multiplexes we go to are separate corporate chains that Paramount (Viacom) has to negotiate with to place a film for exhibition.

Because of this, there is always an indelible pressure on the major studios (production) to make films that exhibitors want to show and an audience wants to see. In many cases that means shorter films and shorter movie trailers with less spoilers. It has nothing to do with our (audience) expectation as much as it has to do with the profit motives of exhibitors. Exhibitors want to fill as many seats as possible (within a given time frame). So, if they have "Theatre A" and it has 300 seats, they want to be able to have the maximum number of showing in that space in a given day. If you have a longer run time, longer trailers, it is going to prevent that from happening. Long running films like TITANIC (1997) THE RING (2002) or DANCES WITH WOLVES (1990) will cut down on the number of times a given space can provide showings in a given day. Of course, movie exhibitors can counter this by offering the same film in a number of spaces within their theatre at one time.

(Audience member calls out: "Pearl Harbor."

Pearl Harbor. That's right. Run time over three hours.

(Audience member: " Also, they are running more ad time."

I'm not even counting that in the run time

(Audience laughter)

I'm just talking about what we write. You bring up an interesting point because one of the other considerations is product placement within the creative work. This off topic but is defined as the seamless integration of advertising and products into content. I've was at a meeting once it was actually discussed that the script itself was not the best but that it should be considered because of its product placement and merchandising potential. They felt they could figure out a way to make it better and that's another story. But product placement can work within a certain degree. I'm thinking of the film Tom Hank's did when he was stranded on the island after the plane crash.

(Audience member: "Cast Away."

Right-- the motion picture -- CASTAWAY (2000). Does anyone remember the role that FEDEX played in that film? The whole story was framed around a FedEx plane crashing and at the end Tom Hanks delivers a FedEx package that had been with him on the island. Don't know if you remember, the girl looked single and was very pretty. How can you beat that for feel good advertising – FedEx always comes through (no matter what) and maybe there will be a loving relationship there as well. Can't beat that.

I think a film where product placement is not so seamless would be Iron Man (2008) where the cars, pizzas, hamburgers were all too present in the way they were placed within the film.

(Audience laughter)

So there is an indelible pressure in cinema for the final product to be … I'm not going to say fixed, but rather a general understanding of runtime for a particular film. This is not present in literature.

So let me ask… are most of your books 300 pages? 250 pages? About 60,000 to 70, 000 words. Anyone over that? Okay, that's right, you already told me that. Anyone over 400 pages… 100,000 words?

(Audience member raises hand)

I'm not saying that is bad. I love those books painted upon a broad canvass. I mean when you read a good book like that, you can settle in and go with it. You know you are going to be with it for a while… which is great. So all of you, the "plus 300 crowd," I'm speaking to you.

Now you've taken this beautifully written manuscript with character development and everything we are talking about and now you have to squeeze all of it into a little square hole that runs on the average 120 pages of dialogue, description and action. So, there is a challenge there. You have to make choices about how to convert what is contained in the longer literary medium where the spoken word and language are used into a visual medium and context for film. You have to consider different methods to make this happen. Earlier this week we discussed starting your screenplay at the most heightened moment of your novel or as it was titled BEGINNING YOUR SCREENPLAY AT THE END. How would you do this? Short answer. You can accomplish this by showing your story through visual exposition. But that's a different seminar. Let's get back to our subject… Writing great characters (we are back on the title). We all want to write great characters. We all want to write great stories.

Now for the second part of our seminar title "IN THE FIRST TEN PAGES." What's that's mean? It's something you put in the title. But there's a little bit of truth to it. Okay, and here it is. We live in a society and I'm not saying anything you don't already know. It's an "immediate gratification" society where we have come to expect everything "now" through, televisions, portable hand held devices and the cloud. We don't want to go through anything that might take too much time. We want it *now.* We don't want a ***"slow roll"*** or too much process in getting to what we came for. It's the same in story telling. You have to get to it as soon as possible or risk losing your audience.

Although you could probably this afternoon list a multitude of very successful movies that have what I am calling a "slow roll." You know you just kind of pull into them nice and easy through a process of character development and exposition. I'm thinking of films like FORREST GUMP (1994) or 2001 A SPACE ODYSSEY (1968) where you're sitting in the theatre wondering where the story is going. But for our purposes here today, I want you to think about creating the most important elements (including characters) of your script right away… and if you can, in the first ten pages.

YOUR PITCH

Now let's go a step further if we could. I'm sure some of you went to some of the pitch workshops here? And now take your wonderful book and try to pitch your entire idea and manuscript in three or four sentences. They listen and then they tell you "We are interested in your book – we would like to develop it into a screenplay. Do you have a screenplay?" And you answer: "Yes, I have a screenplay." They set up a pitch meeting. Next you find yourself sitting at Warner Brothers or Paramount and someone sitting across a desk or on a couch says "Alright, give me your story." And they are talking about that they want your story in a format of no longer than a minute. Now we are going from one mode of presentation to another. We are going from the "full meal" which is your manuscript/book in its entirety, into the shorter version of the screenplay and then even the more abbreviated form of the pitch. This screenplay is not even in consideration. We are simply talking about and idea. I've heard writers say that they have written a really phenomenal screenplay but they never get the actual script in front of anyone because this missed the pitch. What I mean by that is, the have forgotten the idea and got pulled into mechanical process of writing. Don't forget the idea. It sounds very Zen but it's true. Don't get kidnapped by the screenplay or the novel. Always go back to the idea and the pitch. Let everything emanate from that and be ready to have something in your back pocket at a moments notice. That is "if" they don't like your idea, be ready to pitch them something else.

I will tell you a funny story about a pitch. Well, it's not that funny.

(Audience laughter)

I you had to be there. There was this one writer, kind of a nerdy guy, but very smart and very nice. He underwent a process of research and study of the Apollo moon landings. He researched NASA transcripts of all of the Apollo missions to the moon. Project Apollo was America's effort to land a man on the moon and bring him back before the end of the nineteen sixties. This was a challenge set forth by former President John Kennedy and began what was known in the 1960's as the moon race. It was a competition between the United States and the former Soviet Union to land a man on the moon first. The decade was filled with an array of space missions by both countries focusing on getting there first. In the Cold War era, whomever could land a man on the moon first, would have the upper hand in the propaganda war between the two countries and their respective political ideologies. So, it was very important for each country to get there first, no matter what. In July of 1969, the question was answered when America's Neal Armstrong was the first man to walk on the moon on national television. It was a great achievement for mankind and an even greater propaganda victory for the United States over the Soviet Union.

Now, getting back to the writer and his pitch. He developed a theory that history had got it all wrong and that the Russians had actually landed on the moon first and nobody knew about it because it was covered up. And it was not just idle speculation. This writer had specific transcripts of astronauts communicating with mission control.

(Garbled sound effect)

"Houston we've got a problem." I don't think they actually said that but I'm just trying to act it out for you.

(Audience laughter)

His pitch was to tell a story that would radically change history, as we knew it. His story would be told on a larger than life canvass - - outer space and would be filled with intrigue and mystery. In the late, 1960's a spacecraft is launched from Russia on a journey to the moon and then is never heard of or mentioned again. It was a failed mission and no one not even the Russians knew what happened to the spacecraft. What they could not have known was that the spacecraft landed a man on the moon (a Russian cosmonaut) first – before the United States. A single cosmonaut had crash- landed there but had lost the ability to communicate with the Soviet space agency on earth. The Soviet space agency assumed the spacecraft trajectory had missed the moon and was lost in space. They had no way of knowing that the cosmonaut successfully landed on the moon and (after his supplies and oxygen ran out) died there. America went on to take the trophy in the moon race. The fate of the cosmonaut was never known until several years later when NASA astronauts discovered the Soviet craft as they were exploring the lunar surface. The U.S. policy was to keep the discovery a secret to avoid the embarrassment of erasing such an American achievement. Besides the Russians didn't even know it occurred, so why rock the boat?

A Pretty compelling concept and there was also a backstory that spanned to the end of World War II. So, (this writer) he's ready with his story and has facts to back it up -- all lined up. I mean this guy is pumped.

(Pump sounds – Audience laughter.)

He arrives at the meeting and he has what I thought was an okay script. It was a good script but not a great script. It didn't have any heat. It had intellect but no heat. You know when somebody tells you an idea about such a conspiracy, that they say they can prove, creates interest. I'm interested and wondered if it really happened. The script needed some work but that was not the problem because the script never got read. At the meeting, the producer (no name) asked, "Okay, what'ya got for me?" It wasn't a guy with a cigar in his mouth but it felt that way.

(Audience laughter)

"All right, kid...what'ya got?"

Remember, the entire storyline and concept had to be boiled down into one simple idea. The writer looked the producer and said: "All right, here it is. The Russians landed on the moon first… and nobody knows about it."

The producer responded after a moment: "Who gives a crap. Nobody cares about that. What else you got?"

(Audience sighs)

It was that fast. That was it. Nobody cares about that. Period. And so I said to myself. That pitch, what was lacking in the pitch? Let's blame the writer not the producer because the presentation didn't have the spirit of the original idea. It didn't have it. The writer had cut it down so much, that there was no soul left in it. He was no longer offering him a representation of the full idea – instead a small component of it with no connection to the whole and because of that, it ceased to be interesting. I don't know? I have endeavored to think about what he could have said that would have been more interesting. It's easy for me to stand here today and criticize. But the writer never got the chance to have the script read. Not at that studio anyway and point of it was that what failed there was not the idea. It was the mode of presentation.

With respect to mode of presentation, always ask yourself these questions:

1.   What environment am I presenting this idea in?
2.   How can I make my idea fit that mode?

Is it a Burger King hamburger or is it Wolfgang Puck? In the instance of this moon story pitch, the environment and the presentation were not in sync. The producer was expecting something else. How can you make the idea fit the mode? This is an art into itself. If the producer is looking for the writer to give him a one-line concept presentation – perhaps the writer should make his line a question?

A larger question. Something like this.

Writer: What if I told you something that nobody knows about?
Producer: There's very little I don't know about.
Writer: Okay, who landed on the moon?

Producer: The moon, we landed on the moon? I'm only kid-
        ding… the Americans did… everybody knows that.
        Tell me something I don't know.
Writer: You're wrong… the Russians did and the American's
        lied about it.
Producer: Really…
Writer: …and if they lied about that, what else don't you know?

Maybe that would be enough to peek the interest of the producer to get coverage on the script. Then again, maybe not. At least, the writer in my scenario tried to pull the producer in and then at least get a read. When you pitch you have got to create the mode of presentation that best fits the situation. You select the mode of presentation. Take control of the room. It's your moment and you decide how it's going to be played out – good or bad.

    Now, on to the next mode of presentation – getting your adapted script read.

GETTING YOUR ADAPTED SCRIPT READ

The next mode of presentation would be the reading of your script. You now are getting an initial "read." Producer A, B or C says that they would love to read your script. That's what they will tell you but do you actually believe they will read it? No, the script will be given to a reader for coverage and you hope they see what you see in the story. So now your life and your creation is now being entrusted to someone you haven't even met. You might not even know the producer. But now it's being entrusted to someone else – a third party. And they analyze it on a level that may not have anything to do with your creative idea. It (your idea) will be considered for budget. How many of you are doing period pieces?

(Audience – several hands are raised)

Okay, you can imagine the problem with period, is that it costs more money. You may write a brilliant script but it may get shot down simply because the company where you have submitted it may no want to do period pieces or high budgets. So you look at it and you say "Okay, I'm now presenting my work in a third person mode – in which that third person, I don't know, is going to read and evaluate it." That's where the ten pages come in!

You have got to present the most compelling elements of your characters and story up front. Because they may only read part of it and then turn to the end of your script to see how many pages it is. Now, what does that mean? It means nothing or it means everything. If you write a script (in the proper format) for a feature length film and it's 120 – 130 pages, you're okay. If it's 190, you've got a problem… Houston.

(Audience laughter)

Because they are judging you already and they know all the tricks a writer can use to make a longer script appear to be shorter. Smaller fonts, they know all that. You use standard font and hand them a 150-180 page script, it's already got one strike against it. It communicates to the reader/producer that you are not familiar with the intended medium. That's all it means. Then next thing they do is they look at your script and in those first ten pages they are making assumptions about the entire work. If the characters and story contained within the first ten pages are compelling then reason would dictate that the rest of the script is that way as well. It's like when two people meet in a bar or restaurant, one asks, "Hey what do you do?" and the other says, "I dig ditches." Then the first makes the assumption "Not interesting… I'll move on to someone else."

(Audience laughter)

Reading a script is similar to when two people meet for the first time -- they are investing in the first ten minutes (pages)… and within those ten minutes they make a decision about the other person – whether they want to know more about them or not. In the case of your script, they do the same thing—they make assumptions right from the start and decide whether or not to go further. And that's the way people are. It has nothing to do about being good or bad – they are all in hurry to have an answer. That's what they are paid to do. Have an answer. It doesn't mean, that they won't absolutely read the rest of your script if they don't like the beginning. They probably will and do. But you want to be at least at "zero" in the beginning. Zero is that absolute place where it all begins with no prejudice at all upon what you have written. But you don't want to be a t below zero – that's having someone reading your script feeling that it is a chore and that they would rather be doing something else. You want to be at least at zero or better when they start off believing your work has possibilities. This is good. This is good. You want them to keep reading and stead of saying to themselves (this sucks) and then skimming the rest to the end. If your best material is on page fifty-five –they may never truly get there. When that happens, you have lost.

I'm into simplicity. But I want the best (most compelling) parts first. Yesterday, we did an entire hour about starting your screenplay at the end. That was about starting your story at the most intense moment and then filling in the details through exposition. It's a heightened sense of reality. Isn't that what Alfred Hitchcock once said: "Drama is life… with the dull parts cut out." The same applies to the development of your characters. Get to their high point right away – put a mongoose and a cobra face to face right at the start and then show us what can happen. Then give them the rest of the story as you go. Then at least the audience is with you; they are at the party, on the bus, on the train. Whatever analogy you want to use. And they will take the journey with you. Now remember, just because you have written compelling characters doesn't mean it's a sure thing.

Now your script may not make the cut for reasons beyond your control. Reasons that have nothing to do with the quality of your writing including they may not have the budget, the may be looking for a certain type of project (that yours is not) or they may have a specific cast in mind that it doesn't fit. You can't control all the variables but at least you got the read and you can "live to fight / write another day." You will have more manuscripts and next time (now that you have a relationship) you will have something they want. I also, am a believer that the universe will provide. Sometimes you really want something to happen and when it doesn't you become discouraged only to learn that something even better awaits you just around the corner.

(Audience laughter)

My point here is to front load your work as much as you can to compel or propel your reader (whatever term you like) to consider your work and give it their fullest attention.

That's why we say WRITING GREAT CHARACTERS IN THE FIRST TEN PAGES.

In all honesty, no one is counting if you introduce the strongest most compelling elements of character fully by eleven or twelve pages. It's okay. The importance is that it is at the front. Now let's get to one more mode of presentation. You're sitting in the theatre and your book or screenplay has been made into a movie. See it, you're sitting in a darkened theatre as the credits roll... everyone is going to say here... yeah I wish.

(Audience laughter)

ALWAYS PUT YOURSELF IN THE AUDIENCE

A couple of things had to happen. Somewhere along the line, your 250-300-page novel was squeezed into a screenplay. Either you wrote the script or someone else did. So, choices had to be made. What to include what to leave out, then the shooting script was interpreted by a director, later an editor and star. Your original work may have been changed dramatically to fit into the movie you are about to watch. And you are thinking, "My name is on it… what if it's terrible?" The creation of film is a collaborative art and you hope you have a good director, editor and actors. But assuming they are all very talented and you are there (in the theatre) and after the opening credits – the story begins. The same rule applies, within the first ten minutes of the film; the audience needs to be connected to the main characters and story.

In the first two minutes of JURASSIC PARK (1993) the audience sees and hears the menacing velociraptor as it's cage is brought in by a forklift. We don't actually see the whole dinosaur, we just see it's eye and that's really all we need. We're hooked and have to stay to find out what is going to happen.

All this in happens in less than ten minutes. I'm using the number 10 again. Within the first ten minutes of the exhibition of the movie the audience should have an idea of who the main characters are and they should know something about them. And if they don't, there's a problem. Now the velociraptor is certainly not the main character for this story, but it is a pivotal force within the story and frames the main characters the audience meets shortly after this scene. This is essential character development and story telling.

How many times have you been to the movies or a play and you are watching it but you really don't know who the characters are or what it's about? Has anyone ever been there?

(Audience reaction – "Yes")

And then there are examples when an audience can know too much – and they are board seeing what they already know played out over and over again. And then there's the Goldilocks scenario – when it's all just right. Not too little, not too much... just right. That's where you want to be.

Have any of you seen the movie DOUBT (2008)? All right, it was a good movie and within the first three setups of the film – the sermon scene delivered by the late Philip Seymour Hoffman – about two or three minutes into the film, we are introduced to Sister Aloysius played by Meryl Streep. As the sermon is given, she walks quietly down the aisle (we haven't seen her face yet) behind a young boy who is horsing around and slaps him in the back of the head. She then continues walking silently down the isle (as the sermon continues) and comes upon a young boy leaning forward in the pew with his head buried into his arms – he is sleeping. It is here that we finally get our first glimpse of Sister Aloysius's face when she snaps at the lad and whispers "Straighten it!" The boy jumps back to his seat in attention. After that moment, she stands straight and upright and we get a full view of her face. In a few short moments, the audience has been connected to this character and we can imagine that a lot of the pull comes from Streep's performance – but she is working as an actor creating a character within the framework of the writer.

When I say the audience has to know about your character in the first ten pages, I'm not saying they have to know their social security number or anything like that. They have to know the important aspects of your character – so much so that they want to learn more and make the journey.

What about THE WRESTLER (2008)? Has anyone here seen this film?

(Audience – no replies)

You guys have got to get out more.

It opens with the lead character doing what he does. He's in the ring fighting. It is the same idea as the motion picture DOUBT. You are pulled in to his world and you know right off the bat what's going on with this guy. You might say to yourself: "I have never been a wrestler, so what do I know about that? How can I identify with that?" Right? But you may think about it another way. "But I do know something about being on the ropes or knowing people that have been on the ropes who want to pull themselves out of whatever they are in." We all want change? Change for the better? Don't we? I think so. We all want to make our lives better. So this guy happens to be a wrestler who is fighting for a second chance at his life. We can all understand the desire to change because we want to change. And so, we're on the bus – we've paid our money to take the journey.

(Audience – reaction – agreement)

Let's think about one other example that's new. Any of you see the new film out called THE READER (2008)?

(Audience laughter because no one has seen it)

Really, we should just go to the movies tonight.

(Audience laughter)

Here's the deal. THE READER starts off – I'm not going to tell you the whole story but I will tell you a little. I have a problem with THE READER and will tell you that much. My problem is not so much the film as the way it has been marketed as a Nazi movie. And it is about Nazi's in a very abstract way. It's not a movie in anyway about Nazi's – our favorite villains.

(Audience laughter)

Nazi's are such great bad boys you just love to hate. However, the Nazi element of the film is only an instrument to further the characters. It is not a major part of the plot. It's not about the reader (Kate Winslet) being a Nazi prison guard at all. It is really about how two people come together (I've already said too much) and because they come together, it irrevocably changes their lives. I'm not going to tell you any more because you can find that out when you eventually see it.

Now let's think about the motion picture Titanic (1997). The character that was written as Rose (also played by Kate Winslet), within the reality of the film – was part of an arranged marriage and her life was like that of a bird in a cage. Then she has that short relationship the Jack the artist (played by Leonardo DiCaprio). I'm saying short because it's really only a day and a half and then – the ship—you know -- (points down.)

(Audience laughter)

Right? I mean it wasn't like they were hanging out together for a long time. That's why I picked it. Rose has an affair with an artist, a love affair and he paints her picture in the nude – but it's not about that. What it ***is about... because they (Rose and Jack) were together, Rose's life changed***. And the very last scene of the movie – you see it. I remember reading the screenplay at the end of the movie shows Rose (as the older woman) first throwing the precious stone back into the ocean. I don't know if I would have done that...

(Audience laughter)

So she throws the diamond back into the ocean? What's that about? She could have sold it and got a nice oceanfront condo in Boca... or someplace?

(Audience laughter)

Anyway, she throws the diamond back into the sea. The next time we see her in the present frame, she is lying still in her cabin. And I thought (when I saw the film) is she dead? Did she die after living a full life and is now finally back together with everyone who perished on the Titanic? Or... is she sleeping... in peace? James Cameron, wrote this in his screenplay:

A graceful pan across Rose's shelf of carefully arranged pictures.

Rose as a young actress in California, radiant... a theatrically lit studio publicity shot... Rose and her husband, with their two children... Rose with her son at his college graduation... Rose with her children and grandchildren at her 70th birthday. A collage of images of a life lived well.

THE PAN STOPS on an image filling frame. Rose, circa 1920. She is at the beach, sitting on a horse at the surf line. The Santa Monica pier, with its rollercoaster is behind her. She is grinning, full of life.

We PAN OFF the last picture to Rose herself, warm in her bunk. A profile shot. She is very still. She could be sleeping, or maybe something else.

And so Cameron is saying, Rose had a full wonderful life because of that almost momentary relationship with Jack the artist. And whether she is dead or sleeping is really up to you... and that's where he leaves it. And I thought, two characters come together for a very short period of time (and they do get a lot done).

(Audience laughter)

And because these two characters come together in the way they do changes Rose's entire life. Instead of being forced into an arranged marriage (like a caged bird) she lives a full and wonderful life. In that sense, the last shot of the film visually gave us the entire story in one pan of the camera.

So, here are the modes of expression of character or character frames that can originate from your novel or short story

The Pitch
The Script

Now, one other thing, when you're developing a character. Let's go with the first ten pages. What if you are writing for television? Trying to develop your novel into a television series or mini series? It's different. You don't have to do the whole job in the first ten pages because most characters in television are a slow roll. You will have the opportunity to flesh out characters in smaller parts. But with that said, you still have to create the most important character elements in the pilot. That's the initial episode of a series where the audience is introduced to the main characters and the major framework for the show that is to follow.

Since this lecture was given in 2009, many producers and television outlets have decided to do away with pilots all together and produce a limited version of the series from the start. A production such as HOUSE OF CARDS (2013) initially had a limited number of episodes made available to the Netflix subscribers all at one time. They abandoned the idea of a pilot or serial broadcast.

Network television still uses the serial format, but now in television shows such as THE BLACK LIST (2013) and CHICAGO PD (2014) both on NBC major characters or what the audience perceives as major/regular characters in the show are killed of routinely. The writers develop these characters in the traditional manner and just when the audience thinks they know them, they are eliminated. So, your development of character within this medium again must be front-loaded. Get the most interesting/compelling aspects of your character out there early because you may not have twenty episodes or several seasons to flush them out on the fly. You might think, why spend a lot of time developing a character that you will eliminate? My answer, would you do it any differently in a book? I don't think so. And I think anytime you can engage "pull in" your audience with interesting characters, you should do it. Think of William Shakespeare and characters like the Nurse or the Apothecary in Romeo and Juliet. Think about how Shakespeare presented them within the story. He made them interesting and vital to what was going on. You should do the same.

What if you write for the Internet? You adapt your novel as a serial episodic to be shown in smaller segments on the Internet. In this case, you may be developing this on your own and not writing a script for anyone other than yourself. Does this actually work? I mean in the big picture? Does anyone take anything shot for the Internet seriously? The answer is "yes" and "no" depending upon your production values. If your work looks like it's been shot in your backyard with louse light and sound. No one is going to take it seriously. However, if you spend a little time in creating acceptable production values, you can get a following for your work. As far as character development, that all depends how you present it. If it is serial, then you can do a slow roll a little bit at a time, if it were feature format I would front load the first ten minutes and grab your audience. You can produce your story as a mini series, which is a combination of the two formats. But... what can you really do with it?

Here's what I think. If you get enough traction with it and get lots of visits to your site, that can translate into something tangible that you can cite in a fuller pitch meeting. If your project has a lot of heat, people will take an interest. You could also, produce a nice expanded trailer for your book. This really is a marketing tool, very much like they would do in a movie theatre. Show them "how" the film could be if it were made. Get it off the page and visualize your idea. That's a great topic for another seminar!

(Audience laughter)

So depending upon where or how you present your book and characters you will have to be connected the method in which you present it. This means, that not every presentation of one idea will be the same. You have to connect to and reach your reader or viewer by connecting them to your character. You want them to care what happens next. If you produce it yourself, let's say for the Internet, the outcome will be smaller, but you will have more control. The hardest part, I think in this transition from fiction to film... we have to talk about this.

Fiction... you are the only person writing and when you publish you will work with one person – your editor. And when you get to the television or film medium it becomes truly a collaborative effort – and that could become an issue that can affect the final outcome of the way your project looks. It could actually be better than you ever believed or... it could be worse than your worst nightmare.

Let's say that you are fortunate enough to get your novel into the hands of Anthony Hopkins and he or his designee reads it... then you get it back with notes for certain changes or additions that would have to occur if he were to attach himself to the project. In this case, your writing becomes part of a collaborative effort and you have to be open to that. Also, by the time your novel is transformed into a screenplay and then shooting script (after the input of designers, stars, producers and others) it's going to change and like any relationship – you have to give and take a little bit. But you have to make sure that you don't lose your way and your final script doesn't become something else. You'll say that's not what I wrote. But by that time, it will be too late.

One of my plays was produced in (I'm not going to say the name to protect the guilty). It was a fully professional production that's all I will say. When I read the reviews – it got great reviews. It is a tale of father and daughter jealousy and cruelty. The father becomes so jealous of his daughter (both are painters) that he breaks her hands in a paint box so she cannot paint anymore. Despite this, she goes on and become s a world famous artist. The play takes place at her mother's funeral when she (now a famous painter who has gone dry) comes home (from Paris) and sees her father (now an old man) for the first time. Without telling you the whole story, the old man wants her to forgive him for what he has done to her. At the end of the play, she cannot but does understand why he did what he did. She goes back to Paris understanding why he did what he did and is able to paint again. I didn't write it this way… it's better than that.

(Audience laughter)

The producer of the play thinks "We can't have that at the end of the production. She has to forgive him and send the audience out the door feeling good about what they saw." So in that production which I will not name, the ending was changed and she forgives her father and takes him back to Paris with her! So now I'm reading the reviews, which said something, like "The play Autumn Sweet is a poignant drama but chokes at the conclusion with a "Hollywood" ending." I said to myself "I didn't write that!"

(Audience laughter)

The producer changed the ending of my play and I got nailed for it. Why? Because I was on a ski trip in Tahoe instead of being where I should have been. At the opening of my play. I was invited but did not go.

(Audience laughter)

The point of this story is that you need to go with the flow – collaborate – but stay true to your core idea, your characters, and your story. Yes, give and take but not to the extent that you lose your original idea or in my case the ending.

ADAPTATION – YOUR FIRST TEN SCRIPT PAGES

Description, Action and Dialogue

You may be writing for a reader, a producer or an audience and you have got to give. And I've we stated before, that's where the ten pages come in. you have to create a hook in the beginning and once they are on board, they you can roll out any way you need to roll out. How do you get to this with character? Three ways. **Description, Action and Dialogue**. Essentially on the screen that boils down to what they do what they say, how they look, and what other characters say about them and the physical world they exist within. Your main character may say wonderful things about themselves, but they could be telling a lie. You have to show the truth. Let's talk about **DESCRIPTION**.

So, how is the best way to describe your characters in those first ten pages where your character has their initial introduction to the story? Right? So, you have to introduce them in a compelling way. In your novel you could and can take all the time you need. Went to boarding school in France, studied law – add little anecdotes. You don't have that much time and space in a screenplay. You have to cut to the chase.

INTERIOR – LIBRARY – DAY

Professor Muldoon, a crusty but benign college professor, dressed in tweed and loafers, holds an old book tightly as he hobbles down a long oak stairway into the the living room of the old English manor.

You do it all in one to three lines not a page and a half. That's it, you have to create the same impact that you would generate in a page and half description you might have in your novel. And Anthony Hopkins acts it out.

(Audience laughter)

Let's talk about that. Shall we? In your novel you have every detail covered so that you know who the characters are in every detail. Now you've got a screen-play and its all got to be in there but at around 120 pages. So you cut, but you don't want to strip everything out of it. You must capture the essence of your full character description that's in your book. What I'm saying is that you must keep the soul of your book alive and you get that 50 or 100 word description and you boil it down to five or ten words and that's the challenge. But, don't be a good soldier that writes their screenplay in 100 pages but in doing so; the end product has no life in it. You must keep the soul of your book alive and so you struggle to make sure you get in those five or ten lines of description that you don't lose any calories. It has to have the same fullness. The next element is ACTION.

Action is how your character moves in the space – the universe you have cre-ated for them. You don't have to be like "He walked slowly put one foot after an-other." You don't have to do that. Instead focus on something interesting about how your character does something. Some sort of interesting action that they do like the way they tie their tie (James Bond) pet a cat (The Godfather) or walk on a sidewalk (Jack Nicholson in AS GOOD AS IT GETS). But you can create action as it happens "on the fly" as your character does it. Do you remember the old television series COLUMBO (1968)?

(Audience laughter)

I can't believe you guys remember that? Okay, well you would want to put a little bit about that character's actions in your set up. And Detective Columbo was interesting to us because we always enjoyed the way he seemed to physi-cally fumble through each situation he was in. There was a "fumbling" almost inept quality about the character that made his adversaries not take him very seriously. They though "this guy is a total dork." But we loved to see Columbo fumble through and solve every crime despite how carefully it was planned. Sherlock Holmes is the flip side, the Victorian side. Holmes is very formal, scientific and he observes using his five sense everything intently. All his fastidious actions come into play, So action is important because it shows something about your character's way of existing physically in their universe that makes them interesting and worthy of our time. And we can go through all sorts of things to achieve that. It could be that your character in the first ten pages – their relationship with another characters shows....

(Off stage Voice)

Ten minutes? Are you sure?

(Audience laughter)

In the writing class we did yesterday, we were improvising about the "space between people." Just the space can change the way your characters react to things within their universe. You know those people in New York City on the subway? The subway car is packed – standing room only – and they are this far away from one another.)

(Catalano moves very close to a male audience member – almost touches)
(Audience laughter)

Don't worry, I won't touch you...

(Audience laughter)

Unless you want me to?

(Audience laughter.)

They are this far away and it's not a problem. Try that in Los Angeles. Try to move that close to someone and see what happens. I was on line the other day at a store (waiting to check out) and some guy (who was in a hurry) came up right behind me. He very close, I could feel him breathing on me and pressing up against my butt.

(Audience laughter)

No nothing like that... he was (I assume) trying to get the line to move faster. I turned to him and said pressing up against me is not going to make the checkout person or the line any faster. He just moved back... no comment. Now the definition of personal space in Los Angeles and now is different let's say than riding the subway in New York City during the rush hour. This guy pressing up against me in line was a violation of my personal space while it might not have even been noticeable in another situation. Definition of space in Ohio, Los Angeles is different than in New York City, Tokyo or Paris. You can create visual element for your character before they even say one word. This really goes to my example of Meryl Streep in DOUBT. That kind of visual introduction says something about your character and how they move – that might take you several pages to achieve in a novel.

I recently attended a screening of the film CHEF (2014) that (without giving anything away here) is about a chef. The opening sequence of the film (as music plays) is a series of visual shots our main character preparing food – doing the slicing, dicing – all the things a chef would do. But this action was not casual, he was preparing with a sense of purpose – so you knew right away, even before the first word of dialogue was spoken that the meal he was preparing was an important one. He wasn't just cooking breakfast for himself... it was more than that – much more. You'll have to see the film, because you're not getting anything else out of me on CHEF. Have any of you seen it?

(Audience laughter)

Really, we should stop right now and all go to the movies!

(Audience laughter)

But we can't can we? Can we? So you want to open with your characters up front and make them interesting and compelling within that first ten pages or ten minutes of screening. You want the reader/audience to want to know more about them and why they are doing what they are doing. So ACTION is very important tool for you to use to connect your characters to your audience. The other element that is important is of course DIALOGUE.

DIALOGUE is important because it is one the ways (probably one of the most important) a character communicates with an audience and other characters in your story. Dialogue is one of the primary ways your audience gets to know all the things they need to know to be connected to the story. Also, dialogue can reveal things about the character themselves; do they have a dialect, what do they say about themselves, what do they say about others, are they always telling the truth or do they lie? How do they speak? Do they speak in shortened phrases like?

(Catalano does Joe Pesci imitation from Good Fellas (1990)

"You said I was funny? Funny like I'm a clown, I amuse you? I make you laugh? I'm here to amuse you? What do you mean funny, funny how? How am I funny?"

(Audience laughter)

That's one way of doing it. Or does your character speak in long-winded speeches like let's say Sherlock Holmes. Figure out how what they say and how they say it fits in to what you are trying to accomplish.

You can ask my brother just one simple question and he will go off for an hour or more on it. So, really, I don't like asking him anything… you know.

(Audience laughter)

"Hey, Bro… "I call him "Bro" which is term of endearment. "How was your day?" Then he looks at me and smiles as if to say I so glad you asked. "Well, I got up this morning, brushed my teeth and then after that…" I think to myself… please just the highlights – do you have to tell me everything?

Is this your character? So, how they speak dialogue is just as important as exposition and content. When you finally finish the introduction of your main character, I am assuming that your main character is going to be there. Right? So your character walks in and I don't know we were doing THE SOPRANOS yesterday. I kind of dressed for it today. Your character walks in on page two and speaks for the first time with a Jersey dialect: "How ya'doin?"

(Catalano moves)

And he moves within the space leading with chin and is hunched over a bit (like he's going to whisper something important in your ear) or your main character could be an attorney with a physically that is more upright (morally driven)

(Catalano moves again this time more upright and driven.)

"How are you today?"

No chest, no chin. Little details like play strongly or should I say visually. You bring over the characteristics of your novel but with less stated. You keep your character's quality; you don't lose it with abbreviation. It's just as detailed but the detail has been compressed into Description, Action and Dialogue. Guess what? All of these elements are visual and auditory. You have moved from an intellectual medium (your novel) where everything is happens and is created in your head (your imagination) to a primarily visual medium based in external stimuli.

So, you wouldn't say your character enters leading with his chin and right foot. This type of physicality is too clinical. You might instead describe it using visual metaphors. Something like "Joey G walks in the room like a predator ready to strike with his eyes focused on the prize." The metaphor compresses it all into one short section and you can come up with a much better metaphor than I just made up on the spot.

(Audience laughter)

Then, the cinematographer, actors and directors can see it as you see it (from your words) and use their own creative input to interpret it. You might be thinking, what if they interpret my writing in a way that is different than my interpretation? Interpretation is never going to be exact. You aren't going to like this, but often the different interpretations make the impact of the work better. As we have said before, as long as the spirit of your original work is intact, you're okay. And that's what you want to set up in the first ten pages.

WRAPPING IT UP

Ultimately, you want to introduce your characters in an interesting way and as soon as possible (that is a plot device) put them in some sort of peril or heighten the stakes.

This is what I liked so much about the film I won't tell you about – you know THE CHEF (2014). The stakes are heightened right from the first minutes of the film. I was pulled into the main characters almost immediately. Also think about the other examples we've mentioned like JURASIC PARK – you know within the first three or four minutes of the film that this is going to be one rocket ride of a story and character. Make the reader fall in love with your characters and then put them in peril. Threaten to take them away and then you have the whole script to get them out of it.

Never forget your audience. Pull them in as soon as possible and take them on a journey. Whatever you do, don't save the best for last. Not going to work here. Don't roll out the most compelling elements of your characters in the intermission or act break – do it up front. Remember, we live in a society where everyone wants it right away. Some writers even do it in the first page! Novelists do it as well. They create very compelling characters on the first page – so someone picking up the book for the first time will hesitate to put it down. Also, remember film and television are visual mediums – a director will want to show your story more than they will want to tell it. Your screenplay will be blocked into a series of visual setups – focused for a visual telling of the story on a screen.

In your first ten pages that, hook the reader right up front with a heightened reality. If you don't get them up front – you may not be able to get them later.

Thank you very much.

(Audience applause)

www.ingramcontent.com/pod-product-compliance
Lightning Source LLC
Chambersburg PA
CBHW060625030426

42337CB00018B/3208